MINING IN AMERICA

MINING POLICY

BY MARNE VENTURA

Cover image: President Joe Biden signs proclamations on October 8, 2021, to protect national monuments in Utah from mining.

Core Library

An Imprint of Abdo Publishing
abdobooks.com

abdobooks.com

Printed in the United States of America, North Mankato, Minnesota.
052023
092023

THIS BOOK CONTAINS
RECYCLED MATERIALS

Cover Photo: Chip Somodevilla/Getty Images News/Getty Images
Interior Photos: Lewis Hine/Library of Congress/Interim Archives/Archive Photos/Getty Images, 4–5; Red Line Editorial, 7, 33; Kheartmanee Thongyot/Shutterstock Images, 8; Universal History Archive/Universal Images Group/Getty Images, 10, 18–19; David Goldman/AP Images, 12–13, 34–35, 45; Heritage Art/Heritage Images/Hulton Archive/Getty Images, 15, 43; Smith Collection/Gado/Archive Photos/Getty Images, 21; Bettmann/Getty Images, 23; AP Images, 26–27; Rob Carr/AP Images, 28; Biophoto Associates/Science Source, 31; Leigh Vogel/Stringer/Getty Images Entertainment/Getty Images, 37; Diane Desobeau/AFP/Getty Images 39

Editor: Angela Lim
Series Designer: Ryan Gale

Library of Congress Control Number: 2022949082

Publisher's Cataloging-in-Publication Data

Names: Ventura, Marne, author.
Title: Mining Policy / by Marne Ventura
Description: Minneapolis, Minnesota: Abdo Publishing Company, 2024 | Series: Mining in America | Includes online resources and index.
Identifiers: ISBN 9781098290979 (lib. bdg.) | ISBN 9781098277154 (ebook)
Subjects: LCSH: Mines and mining--Juvenile literature. | Mines and mineral resources--Juvenile literature. | American history--Juvenile literature. | Mining engineering--Juvenile literature. | United States--Juvenile literature.
Classification: DDC 622.0973--dc23

CONTENTS

CHAPTER ONE

EXPLOSION!

It was a typical morning at the Monongah coal mine in West Virginia. At 10:00 a.m. on December 6, 1907, the underground tunnels were full of workers. Many of the miners were young boys. Suddenly, an explosion in one of the tunnels caused the entrance of the mine to cave in, preventing fresh air from flowing into the mine. Then, a larger blast rocked a second tunnel. The collapse trapped toxic gases in the underground mine. More than 350 miners

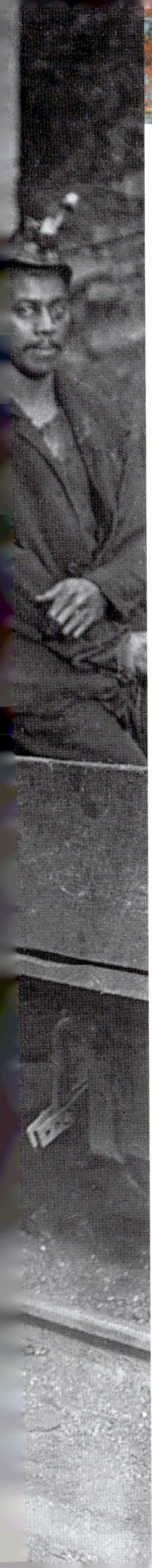

Coal mining has been a part of West Virginia's economy since the 1810s.

were killed in the disaster. Some were crushed by the collapse. Others died from lack of air or breathing in the poisonous fumes.

Mining accidents were common at the time. But this was the worst mining disaster in US history. People called on the US government to help. They asked lawmakers to put rules in place to keep miners safe. In 1910, the government created the US Bureau of Mines (USBM). This agency is made of a group of experts who work together to come up with solutions to protect miners and prevent mining accidents.

COAL

Coal is the most commonly mined material in the United States. It is used as fuel to make electricity. Power plants burn coal to heat water and make steam. Steam drives generators that create electricity. In 2022, approximately 23 percent of US electricity was made by coal-fired power plants. Coal is also used to make steel, cement, carbon fibers and foams, medicines, and tars. Coal can be used as fuel for heating homes and offices.

MINING DISASTERS
IN THE UNITED STATES

The chart below shows information about some of the worst mining disasters in US history. Study the chart. What caused most of the mining deaths? The US Bureau of Mines was created in 1910. What kinds of policies could the agency have put into effect to prevent these disasters?

Date	Location	Effects
December 1, 1907	Naomi Mine in Fayette City, Pennsylvania	An explosion caused by gas, an open flame, and coal dust killed 34 miners.
December 6, 1907	West Virginia Mine in Monongah, West Virginia	Explosions in the underground tunnels killed more than 350 miners.
December 19, 1907	Darr Mine in Westmoreland County, Pennsylvania	An explosion in the underground tunnels and rooms killed 239 men and boys.
November 13, 1909	Cherry Coal Mine in Cherry, Illinois	A fire burned support beams in the mine, trapping and killing 259 miners and rescuers.
December 21, 1951	Orient No. 2 Mine in West Frankfort, Illinois	An explosion inside the mine tunnel killed 119 miners.
November 20, 1968	Consol No. 9 coal mine in Farmington, West Virginia	An explosion killed 78 miners.

The United States ranks third in annual coal production, behind China and India.

MINING

Mining is the process of removing minerals and other materials from the ground. Coal, gold, and iron ore are examples of mined materials. To get these materials, miners may dig holes or tunnels that go deep underground. This is called underground mining. Other mines are huge open pits. These are surface mines. Today, many of the everyday products people use contain mined materials. Pencils, baking soda, glass, plastics, kitchenware, batteries, cars, and computers are all made from mined materials.

Mining can be dangerous. Accidents can trap workers underground. Mining equipment and explosives can be unsafe. Materials such as coal can make dust that causes health problems.

PERSPECTIVES

THE FUTURE OF COAL

Coal is burned to create heat and energy. But burning coal releases gases that have caused Earth's average temperature to rise over the years. This is called climate change. Climate change is harmful to life on Earth. It causes changes in weather patterns such as more frequent droughts and flooding. Some experts want other sources of energy such as wind, solar, and nuclear power to replace coal and other fossil fuels. Energy researchers Robert B. Finkelman, Amy Wolfe, and Michael S. Hendryx wrote, "The role that [burning coal] plays in contributing to global warming and climate change . . . demands the end of coal use."

Miners had to handle dangerous explosives to extract ores.

Mining can also harm the environment.

For these reasons, the US government creates mining policies to protect workers and the environment.

Mining policies are the set of rules the government has made to make the mining process safer. After its establishment, the USBM led the way in researching ways to make mining safer. It required inspections of mines for health and safety. It also discovered more efficient ways to mine. The work of the USBM and other government programs has greatly influenced US mining policies.

EXPLORE ONLINE

Chapter One introduces some of the benefits and risks of mining. How is mining helpful to people? What are some harmful effects of mining? Read the article at the website below. How does the information on the website support the information in Chapter One? Does the website present any new information?

MINING

abdocorelibrary.com/mining-policy

CHAPTER TWO

EARLY MINING POLICIES

Early mining policies addressed where people could mine and basic safety. The Mining Law of 1872 was the first US law about mining. It gives US citizens the right to mine for minerals on federal lands. This law helped the mining industry grow. It is still in effect today.

In 1891, the first federal law about mine safety was passed. It set minimum airflow standards in underground coal mines. Good airflow helped move harmful gases out of

Some miners today operate mining machinery underground. Mining policies make sure miners are kept safe.

the tunnels. The law also banned children younger than 12 from working in mines.

During this time, many Americans were also concerned about conservation. They wanted to protect land and water from pollution. In 1896, the Federal Department of Mines was created to reduce the effect of mining on the environment.

COAL MINE EXPLOSIONS

Coal mine explosions have two main causes: methane gas or coal dust. When coal is mined, methane is released. Heat from machinery can cause the gas to explode. Coal dust explosions can be triggered by methane explosions. The wind from methane explosions stirs up coal dust, and the heat makes the coal dust explode. To prevent explosions, mine operators use large fans to make the methane less dense. Mine operators also drill holes to let methane flow out of the mine. They spray water to cool hot equipment.

THE USBM

Several mining disasters in the early 1900s made Congress aware of the need for better safety policies. In 1907 alone, mining accidents killed more

In the 1910s, USBM researchers conducted experiments to help improve mineral extraction and mining safety.

than 3,000 people. President Theodore Roosevelt recommended that Congress create an agency to regulate mining.

In 1910, the role of the Federal Department of Mines expanded. It became the USBM. Its first goals were to find safer blasting materials for mines and to prevent mine explosions. The USBM also worked to set up ways to rescue miners after a disaster. It trained rescue workers in first aid. The USBM bought railroad cars for use in mine rescue missions. The rescue train cars held first aid equipment and were staffed by rescue workers. The workers were prepared to quickly arrive at the scene of an accident.

The USBM provided safety guidelines. But it did not have the authority to inspect mines. The USBM could not force mine operators to follow its guidelines. In 1941 and 1947, new laws gave federal inspectors the right to enter mines and check for safety. They could notify mine operators if they were breaking safety rules. The USBM had made major improvements in mining safety. But it still had a long way to go. It needed laws that would allow it to enforce safety rules.

PERSPECTIVES

MINE SAFETY DEMONSTRATIONS

To raise awareness about mine safety, USBM rescue teams gave demonstrations in Pittsburgh, Pennsylvania, in October 1911. The rescue teams showed people how to give first aid. They showed how to use devices that improve the flow of air in underground mines. President William Taft came. He gave Red Cross medals to rescue team captains. He spoke of the importance of being prepared: "We must stamp out the spirit of carelessness and the happy-go-lucky idea that I am afraid is too common with Americans generally."

STRAIGHT TO THE SOURCE

President Theodore Roosevelt spoke about the need to create the US Bureau of Mines. In a 1907 speech to Congress, he said:

> *A bureau of mines should be created . . . to collect statistics and make investigations in all matters pertaining to mining and particularly to the accidents and dangers of the industry. If this cannot now be done, at least additional appropriations should be given [to] the Interior Department to be used for the study of mining conditions, . . . for carrying on the work of mapping the mining districts, for studying methods for minimizing the accidents and dangers in the industry; in short, to aid in all proper ways the development of the mining industry.*

Source: "Theodore Roosevelt: State of the Union 1907 – 3 December 1907." *American History*, n.d., let.rug.nl. Accessed 20 Sept. 2022.

POINT OF VIEW

President Roosevelt believed the creation of the US Bureau of Mines was necessary. What does he say should be the main goals of the agency? Read back through this chapter. Do you think there are other issues the USBM should address?

CHAPTER THREE

CHILD LABOR, WAGES, AND HOURS

Child labor in the United States was common from the late 1800s until 1938. Many families relied on their children to help pay for basic needs, such as food and shelter. Some people thought it was important for children to learn a trade at a young age. They believed it was necessary to teach children the value of hard work.

Other people disagreed about whether children should work. Some jobs were dangerous. Those who wanted to ban child

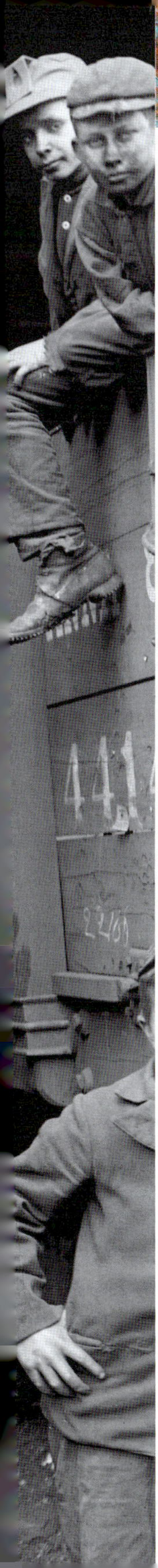

Around 1890, workers at the Woodward Coal Mines in Pennsylvania included young boys.

PERSPECTIVES

CHILD LABOR REFORM

Between 1902 and 1906, people who opposed child labor began to write articles for the public to read. More and more people began to agree that young children should not be working in mines. But some parents and even their children disagreed with the reformers. These parents said they needed the wages their children earned to live. In one Pennsylvania mining town, the head of the school found that nearly 200 school-age boys were working in the mines. Some had parents who had faked doctor's notes to excuse their children from school. The parents did this so their boys could work in the coal mine.

labor pointed out the dangers of mining. Many children were hurt or killed in mining accidents. Children who worked in mines did not go to school. They lost the chance to get an education. This meant that as adults, they might not be able to get a job outside the mining industry.

1902 COAL STRIKE

Mining was difficult and dangerous in the early 1900s. US mine operators often

Miners gathered outside a building in West Virginia in 1938. They waited to collect their paychecks.

brought in workers from other countries who were willing to work for lower wages than local miners. This meant there were fewer jobs for American miners. In 1902, miners were paid very little. One report says a miner got $1.60 for a ten-hour workday, or 16 cents per hour. Today, that would be about $4.50 per hour. The federal minimum wage in 2022 was $7.25 per hour.

Such low wages made it hard for miners to support their families.

The United Mine Workers of America (UMWA) formed in 1890. The UMWA is a union that still operates today. A union is made of workers within an industry. The workers band together to protect their rights. In May 1902, UMWA leaders asked to meet with mine operators in Pennsylvania. They wanted higher pay and shorter hours. The mine operators refused to meet with them.

YOUNG MINERS

In US mines, young children worked as trappers, breakers, or helpers. Underground mines have wooden doors that allow air to flow into and out of the tunnels. Trappers opened and closed these doors to let coal cars enter and exit the mine. Breakers sat on wooden benches next to moving belts. The moving belts carried mined materials. The breakers' job was to break up the material and separate the coal. Dust from the broken coal could get so thick that it was hard to see. Helpers typically performed jobs such as loading coal into cars.

A group of coal miners went on strike in 1975. They wanted to protect their right to protest without the risk of being stopped by a court order.

The miners went on strike. They hoped this would force the mine operators to meet their demands.

The mine shutdown caused a shortage of coal in the eastern United States. People could not heat their homes without coal. President Theodore Roosevelt wanted to help solve the problem. He felt it was his duty to help. Roosevelt was also worried that the dispute between the workers and mine operators could lead to riots. The president called a meeting with the mine operators and UMWA leaders. In past strikes, US presidents tended to side with employers.

They sent in soldiers to break up the strikes. This marked the first time in US history that a president served as a neutral peacemaker. At first, the mine operators still refused to meet the demands of the union. Roosevelt responded by forming a group of experts to listen to both sides and find a solution. Finally, the operators and union workers reached an agreement. The miners got a 10 percent pay raise. They would work nine hours each day instead of ten. This was a turning point in US policy.

THE FAIR LABOR STANDARDS ACT OF 1938

The 1902 coal strike led to better working conditions for miners. But it was not until 1938 that US policies about labor changed for all industries. President Franklin D. Roosevelt signed the Fair Labor Standards Act in 1938. This federal law set a minimum age for child labor. Children under the age of 16 were not allowed to work in jobs outside their homes. No child under the age of 18 was allowed to work in a dangerous job. The secretary of labor determined that mining was a dangerous job.

The Fair Labor Standards Act also set the minimum wage at 25 cents per hour. Today that is equal to a $5.25 hourly wage. The maximum workweek was set at 44 hours. If workers spent more than 44 hours per week at their job, they were required to receive overtime pay from their employers. Overtime pay is 1.5 times the hourly wage.

FURTHER EVIDENCE

Review Chapter Three. What is the main point of the chapter? Name two or three supporting details for the main point. Now read the article at the website below. Find a quote that supports the main point of this chapter. Does the quote repeat any supporting details?

CHILD LABOR

abdocorelibrary.com/mining-policy

MINE

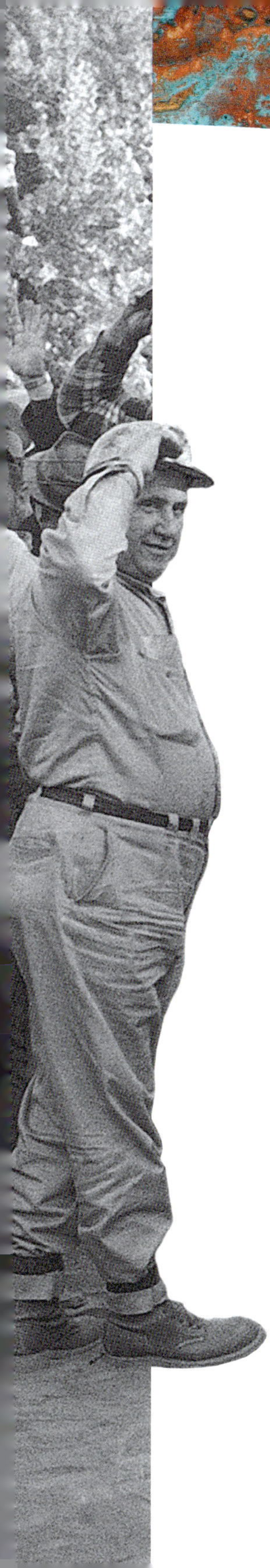

CHAPTER FOUR

HEALTH AND SAFETY

Working in mines was a dangerous job. Old mine roofs and supporting structures could collapse. Air vents could close unexpectedly. Gases in the mine exploded if exposed to heat.

On December 21, 1951, an underground explosion in West Frankfort, Illinois, killed 119 miners. The disaster took place at the Orient No. 2 Mine. Before the explosion,

Miners at work in Hazleton, Pennsylvania, celebrated after a successful rescue mission brought two miners who had been trapped underground back to the surface in 1963.

Mines today are routinely inspected to ensure that they follow US regulations.

an inspection led by the USBM found that the mine operators failed to follow 31 mine safety rules. The mining company had ignored the inspectors' recommendations. An official at the USBM said the disaster was avoidable.

In response to this and other mining disasters, Congress passed the Federal Coal Mine Safety Act of 1952. It gave the USBM the right to inspect underground coal mines every year. It also gave the agency the right to report unsafe conditions to mine operators. It could stop the operators from sending miners into unsafe mines. It also gave the federal government the right to shut down mines that were dangerous. In the first year after the act was passed, thousands of coal mine operators made their mines safer to avoid being shut down. They strengthened mine roofs and supporting structures. They stopped using dangerous

THE ABERFAN DISASTER

The village of Aberfan in South Wales was home to a coal mine that opened in 1875. For years, waste from the mine was unsafely dumped into a pile on the side of a mountain above the village. The local government complained to the mine operators about the danger of a mudslide. But the mine company ignored the complaints. On October 21, 1966, a heavy rain caused the waste to slide down the mountain and into the village. It smashed into the grade school. More than 100 schoolchildren died when they were buried in muddy waste that was 40 feet (12 m) deep. The disaster drew worldwide attention to the need for safer mining policies.

blasting powders. They placed fans for better airflow and banned smoking and open flames. They checked mines for gas before miners entered.

HEALTH EFFECTS

Health experts reported that the coal dust miners inhaled caused an illness called black lung disease. This illness starts with coughing, chest pain, and trouble breathing. Over time, it can form scars on the lungs. This makes it hard to get oxygen into the blood, which can harm the heart and brain. Miners suffering from the disease need health care. Many become too sick to work.

Congress passed the Federal Coal Mine Health and Safety Act of 1969. It required four yearly inspections at all underground coal mines. Mine operators were fined or even charged with a crime for not following safety rules. This act was also the first to deal with the health of miners. Under the law, miners who could not work because of black lung disease received

Coal dust builds up in the lungs over time. The black dust can be seen in this section of a coal miner's lung.

money as compensation. The government and mining companies recognized that the miners had become sick because of their work in mines. In addition, the act took steps to reduce the risk of black lung disease. It set levels on how much coal dust was allowed. It required mining companies to perform tests to check the lung health of miners.

Congress added to the 1969 act with the Federal Coal Mine Safety and Health Act in 1977. This law, which is also called the Mine Act, still regulates mining today. The Mine Act created the Mine Safety and Health Administration (MSHA) that focused primarily

PERSPECTIVES

BLACK LUNG DISEASE

A 2021 study by Dr. Robert Cohen of the University of Illinois surveyed coal miners in Appalachia. This region of the United States has many coal mines. The study found that silica dust is causing a rise in black lung disease among coal miners in Appalachia. Silica dust goes into the air when miners cut into sandstone. Cohen wants MSHA to set a limit for how much silica dust miners can be exposed to. Cecil E. Roberts, the president of the United Mine Workers of America, agrees. He says, "I testified before Congress in 2019 on this exact issue and nothing was done. . . . MSHA needs to act to enforce a silica standard to protect today's miners. Failure to act risks the lives of thousands."

on reducing deaths, injuries, and illnesses in mining. The Mine Act gives miners the right to report unsafe conditions and get help with other health and safety issues.

The Mine Act resulted in a major decrease in mining accidents and deaths for many years. But a series of mining accidents in 2006 killed 47 miners. These deaths led Congress to pass new laws for mine safety. The Mine Improvement and New

MAKING PROGRESS

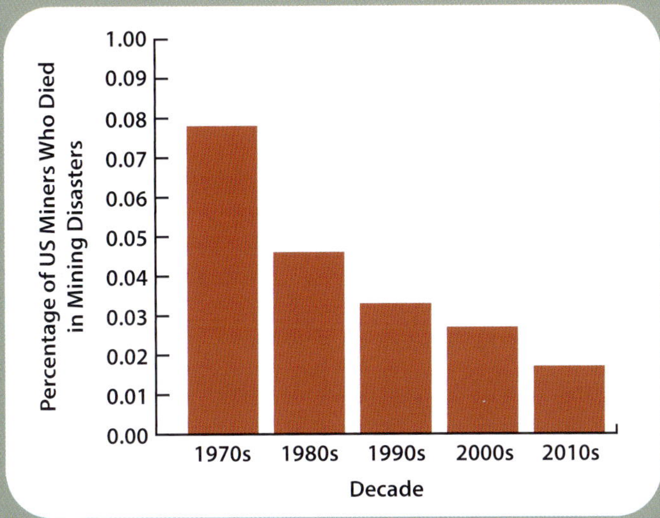

The graph above shows the percentage of US miners who died in mining accidents each decade from 1970 through 2019. Each decade, fewer than 0.1 percent of miners died in mining accidents. How has the number of deaths in mining accidents changed since the Mine Safety and Health Act of 1977?

Emergency Response (MINER) Act was added in May 2006. It required mine operators to have an emergency plan for accidents. Rescue teams must be able to arrive at the mine within one hour of an accident. The MINER Act allowed MSHA to charge as much as $10,000 if mine operators did not follow safety rules. MSHA has the authority to shut down mines if mine operators do not pay the fine.

CHAPTER FIVE

ENVIRONMENTAL POLICIES

The process of mining is harmful to the environment in several ways. Digging pits and tunnels for surface and underground mines can lead to erosion. Soil erosion results in an increased risk of flooding. Waste materials can run into streams and pollute the water, which can be harmful to people and wildlife. The water may no longer be safe to drink. Sometimes gases and mineral particles are released into the air when metals are heated. These are harmful for humans

In addition to protecting the safety and health of miners, government workers inspect how mining affects the environment.

to breathe. In addition, abandoned mines can be dangerous. People might fall into tunnels. Steep areas can collapse.

In the 1960s, Americans grew more concerned with protecting the environment. President Richard Nixon created the US Environmental Protection Agency (EPA) on December 2, 1970, in response. The mission of the EPA is to protect human health and the environment. The EPA is one federal agency that regulates mines to keep the environment safe.

WATER POLLUTION

Rock and soil are broken up when minerals are extracted. This waste material often has small amounts of metals that are harmful to the environment. When waste washes into waterways, it causes the water to have less oxygen. This can kill fish, fish eggs, and other animals and plants in the water. Fish populations may be reduced. The surviving fish may be dangerous to eat.

ACTS THAT REGULATE MINING

Congress passed the Clean Air Act in 1970.

Activists spoke in front of the Supreme Court in 2022 in support of the Clean Air Act. Some coal mining companies wanted to loosen the restrictions established by the act.

This act worked to limit air pollution in the United States. Because of the Clean Air Act, mining industries had to limit the amount of coal dust and waste material they put into the air.

Congress passed two more acts in the 1970s that affected the mining industry. These acts aimed to reduce pollution. The Resource Conservation and

PERSPECTIVES

CLEAN POWER PLAN

In 2015, President Barack Obama suggested a Clean Power Plan. The purpose of the plan was to reduce the use of coal power in the United States. It would limit pollution that leads to climate change. North Dakota sued the EPA to stop the Clean Power Plan. Mining is a major industry in North Dakota. The state won the lawsuit, but the use of coal power still declined in the years that followed. Experts believe this was because other sources of energy such as natural gas were becoming cheaper.

Recovery Act passed in 1976. It makes sure mines safely get rid of solid waste. The Clean Water Act passed in 1977. It manages how mines get rid of water used in the mining process to prevent the pollution of rivers and streams.

In 1980, the Comprehensive Environmental Response, Compensation, and Liability Act was passed. This act gives the government the right to clean up mining sites where waste materials

Mining in the United States is influenced by policy makers who consider the economic benefits of mining and the environmental effects the industry has.

STOP AND THINK

Take a Stand

People disagreed about whether children should be allowed to work during the late 1800s and early 1900s. Some thought it was valuable for children to learn a skill and help pay for their families' expenses. Today's labor policy prohibits children under the age of 14 from working. People must be 18 years or older to work a dangerous job. Do you agree with these age requirements? What do you think the cutoff age should be? Should it be higher or lower?

You Are There

Chapter Three discusses the low wages and long workdays most miners experienced in the early 1900s. Imagine you are working as a miner during the 1902 coal strike. Write a letter to President Theodore Roosevelt. Tell him about how much you are paid and how many hours you work each day. How do your wages and work hours make life hard for you and your family? What would you like the president to do to help?

Another View

This book talks about the health effects caused by mining. As you know, every source is different. Ask a librarian or another adult to help you find a second source about this topic. Write a short essay comparing and contrasting the new source's point of view with that of this book's author. What is the point of view of each author? How are they similar and why? How are they different and why?

Tell the Tale

Chapter One of this book discusses the Monongah mine disaster. Imagine you were near the mine during the time of the explosion. Write 200 words about what you see. How would witnessing this disaster affect your opinions about the need for mining policies?

GLOSSARY

appropriation
money set aside for a specific use

compensation
payment made to injured or sick workers who are unable to work

enforce
to carry out a law and make sure people follow it

extract
to remove a mineral or metal from rock

mineral
a naturally occurring material that is typically found underground

ore
a solid material that often contains metals that can be used

pollute
to make dirty or unhealthy

riot
to create public violence or disorder

statistics
a collection of data that includes numbers

strike
to stop work or service as a way to protest rules or working conditions

ONLINE RESOURCES

To learn more about mining and mining policy in the United States, visit our free resource websites below.

Core Library
CONNECTION
FREE! COMMON CORE MULTIMEDIA RESOURCES

Visit **abdocorelibrary.com** or scan this QR code for free Common Core resources for teachers and students, including vetted activities, multimedia, and booklinks, for deeper subject comprehension.

Booklinks
NONFICTION NETWORK
FREE! ONLINE NONFICTION RESOURCES

Visit **abdobooklinks.com** or scan this QR code for free additional online weblinks for further learning. These links are routinely monitored and updated to provide the most current information available.

LEARN MORE

Dickmann, Nancy. *How We Use Fossil Fuels*. Crabtree, 2021.

Gale, Ryan. *The History of Mining*. Abdo, 2024.

Kaiser, Emma. *Mining and the Environment*. Abdo, 2024.

INDEX

About the Author

Marne Ventura has written more than 100 books for children. She holds a master's degree in education from the University of California. Her favorite topics are nature; science, technology, engineering, and math (STEM); crafts; food; biographies; and health. Marne and her family live in California.